LIVING IN HISTORY

A VICTORIAN SCHOOL

Peter Chrisp

Illustrations by Nick Hewetson

CONTENTS

Produced for Heinemann Children's Reference by
Roger Coote Publishing, Gissing's Farm
Fressingfield, Suffolk IP21 5SH

Educational Consultant: Jane Shuter
Editorial Director: David Riley
Art Director: Cathy Tincknell
Production Controller: Lorraine Stebbing

First published in Great Britain in 1997 by
Heinemann Children's Reference
an imprint of Heinemann Educational Publishers
Halley Court, Jordan Hill, Oxford OX2 8EJ
a division of Reed Educational & Professional Publishing Ltd

MADRID ATHENS PRAGUE FLORENCE PORTSMOUTH NH
CHICAGO SAO PAULO SINGAPORE TOKYO MEXICO
MELBOURNE AUCKLAND IBADAN GABORONE
JOHANNESBURG KAMPALA NAIROBI

ISBN 0431 06826 7 (Hbk)   ISBN 0431 06827 5 (Pbk)

British Library Cataloguing in Publication Data
A catalogue record for this book is available from the British Library.

03 02
10 9 8 7 6 5

Printed in Hong Kong

A Board School of the 1880s

In the nineteenth century, there were several different types of school in Britain. For the rich and the middle classes, there were private schools, which charged fees. But for poor children, especially in the cities, there were few schools. If they were lucky, poor children might go to a school run by the Church. However, many children did not go to school at all, but out to work.

▲ Many country children went to a small village school, like this one. It might be run by a school board, or by one of the churches.

In 1870, the government decided that every child should be able to go to school. New schools were set up all over the country, paid for by government money and local taxes called rates. The schools charged a small fee, though the poorest families did not have to pay anything. They were called 'board schools' because they were run by a 'board', a group of local people, elected by the ratepayers.

▼ The new board schools were mostly built in big towns, where land for building was scarce. As a result, they had to be tall buildings.

At first, parents could decide whether to send their children to school or not. But in the 1870s, the government passed laws to make sure that all children got an education. By 1880 every British child had to go to school until the age of 10.

This book is about one of the many new board schools that were built in the 1870s and 1880s.

WHO'S WHO IN THE SCHOOL?

The Board School was really three different schools in one building. There was an infants' school, which taught boys and girls aged between 3 and 7. Then there was a boys' school and a girls' school, each teaching pupils aged between 7 and 13. Each school had between 500 and 600 pupils.

Each school had its own staff of teachers and headteacher. The teachers in the boys' school were all male. The teachers in the infants' and girls' schools were female. The men were much better paid than the women.

▶ These are the headteachers of the three schools. On the left is the headmaster of the boys' school, in his late 40s. The headmistress of the girls' school, also in her 40s, is in the middle. The headmistress of the infants, in her mid-30s, is on the right.

◀ A young woman teacher waits for a boy in the infants' school to do a sum, using his fingers.

Children older than 7 were divided into six grades called 'standards'. To move from a lower standard into a higher one, they had to come to school regularly and pass an exam at the end of the year. Children who stayed away from school, or kept failing the exam, might never leave Standard One. Hard-working children could jump two standards at once. This meant that children of different ages were often taught in the same class.

Some classes were looked after by older children, called monitors. They were paid a small sum to give out the books and watch over the children as they moved around the school. Much of the care of the infants was left to girl monitors, aged 10 to 12.

At the age of 13, monitors could become 'pupil teachers'. They were studying to be teachers. Pupil teachers taught school lessons and, in the evenings, they were taught by the headteacher. At about the age of 19, they took an exam. If they passed, they became 'assistant teachers'. Then they had to study for yet another exam to become fully qualified teachers. They had to do all this studying in their own time, after they finished work.

▲ A 13 year-old 'pupil teacher' reads to a class of infants.

◀ This girl is an 11 year-old monitor, looking after an infants' lesson.

THE SCHOOL BUILDING

The board school was a big brick building with three floors – one floor for each of the three schools. The infants' school was on the ground floor. The first floor belonged to the boys' school. The girls were taught on the top floor. The boys' school and the girls' school were separate, with their own entrances and playgrounds. After the age of 7, boys and girls were kept apart.

Boys' School

Boys' schoolrooms

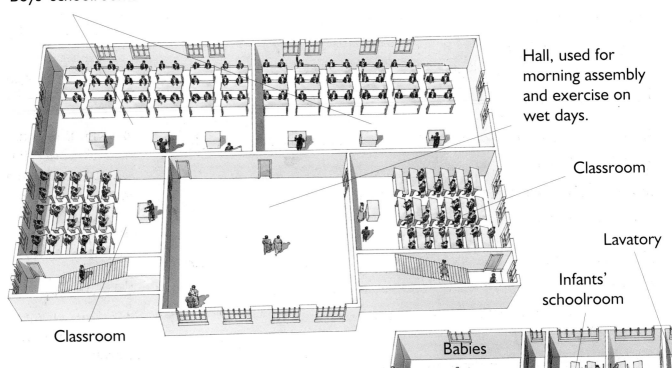

Hall, used for morning assembly and exercise on wet days.

Classroom

Lavatory

Infants' schoolroom

Classroom

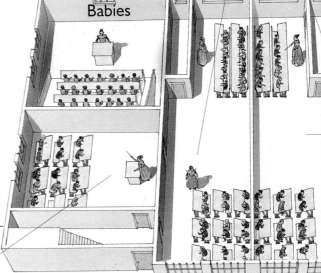

Babies

Classroom

Above is the boys' school. There is a large hall, used for school assembly, and for physical exercise on wet days. On either side of the hall, there is a small classroom, which held a single class of around 70 boys. At the top, there are two big schoolrooms, each shared by three classes.

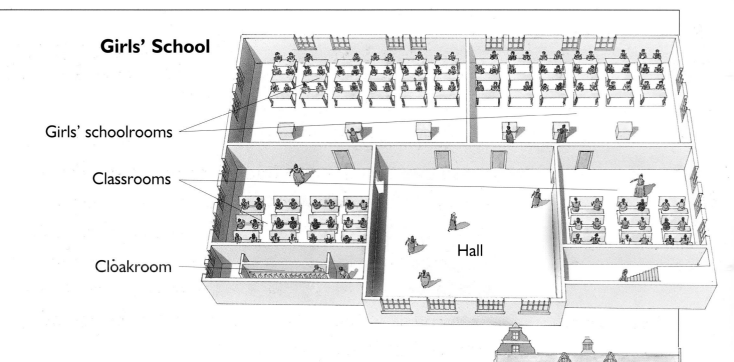

Girls' School

Girls' schoolrooms

Classrooms

Cloakroom

Hall

There were more than 200 boys in each of these rooms. Imagine being taught in a room with three lessons going on at once! Teachers often had to shout to make themselves heard.

Below you can see the infants' school, where boys and girls aged 3 to 7 were taught. Infants under 5 were called the 'babies'. They were looked after by monitors in the two rooms at the top of the plan.

The girls' school, above, has almost the same plan as the boys' school, with two large schoolrooms and two small classrooms. All the rooms in the board school had high ceilings, for good ventilation. The Victorians were very keen on fresh air, to help stop the spread of disease.

▲ On this outside view of the school you can see the big windows, needed to let in plenty of light. They were usually high up the walls, to stop children gazing outside when they should have been studying.

The walls were decorated with coloured prints – maps of the world, showing all the countries then ruled by Britain, pictures of animals, and illustrations of stories from the Bible.

Babies

Infants' schoolroom

Classroom

Infants' School

SCHOOL EQUIPMENT

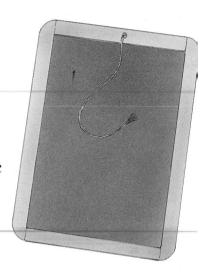

Y ou would probably recognize much of the equipment used in a board school. The teachers wrote on chalkboards, and the children used textbooks and exercise books, just like today.

The younger pupils wrote and drew on a slate using a slate pencil – this faintly scratched the surface, leaving marks which could be wiped out with a wet cloth. Older children wrote in ink, using a wooden pen with a metal nib. Ink was kept in china ink-wells, which were filled each day by a monitor.

▲ A child's writing slate. The string was for tying around a slate pencil.

◀ Pen and ink-wells.

The children sat at desks. Each desk was designed for two pupils. It had a flap, used for writing, which was raised when the child had to stand up. Children were expected to stand whenever a grown-up entered the room, to show respect. They also had to stand up to read a passage or answer questions. A slot at the back of the desk was used for storing the slate, while books could be kept on the shelf underneath. There was a groove on the desk, for a pen or a slate pencil, and a hole for the ink-well.

The school owned many different textbooks, written for children of different ages. There were reading books, called primers, for the infants. These used simple passages with short words: 'My dog is in the bog. My hog is in the bog. My cat is in the bog. My rat is in the bog.' For older children, the textbooks were often in the form of questions and answers: 'Q. What shape is the earth? A. It is nearly round. Q. How do you know that? A. Because ships have sailed round it.'

▼ A sharpener for slate pencils.

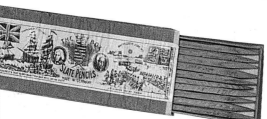

▲ A box of slate pencils.

◄ Children at their desks. They have stored their slates in the slot at the front of each desk.

▶ A typical board school desk. The frame was made of iron, and the other parts were wood.

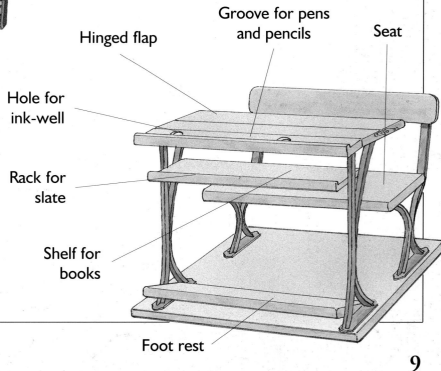

Hinged flap

Groove for pens and pencils

Seat

Hole for ink-well

Rack for slate

Shelf for books

Foot rest

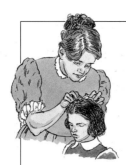

THE BEGINNING OF THE DAY

The school day began at 9 am, when a bell rang to call the children in from the playground. Each of the three schools had its own religious assembly, led by the headteacher. The children said the Lord's Prayer ('Our Father, which art in heaven... '), which they had learned by heart. Then they sang a hymn and listened as the headteacher read from the Bible and spoke about religion.

Religion was an important part of school life. The members of the board of governors, which ran the school, were usually people with strong Christian beliefs. They wanted to make sure that the children became good Christians. Although most British people were Christian at the time, there were also Jewish children in some board schools, especially in the bigger cities. They were allowed to wait in a classroom while assembly was held.

▼ Assembly is under way in the girls' school. The girls stand quietly while their headmistress reads to them from the Bible. She might also talk to them about good behaviour, telling them how important it was that they worked hard and were polite to grown-ups.

◄ These girls are having their heads inspected for ringworm, a type of fungus, and tiny blood-sucking insects called lice. Lice were bad enough on their own, but they could also spread a very dangerous disease called typhus.

After assembly, the 'register', or list of children, was read out by a teacher. Each name was ticked off as the child answered. The amount of money paid by the government to the school depended on the number of children taught. The school gave medals and prizes to encourage children to come every day.

Before lessons could begin, the children were often inspected to make sure they were clean and showed no signs of sickness. Dirty children were sent to the lavatories to wash. The teachers' biggest worry was that a child might arrive with measles, scarlet fever or small-pox. These diseases were much more common than they are today – and they could quickly spread from child to child. They were also more serious. Scarlet fever could kill the children who caught it. A bad outbreak could close down a school for weeks.

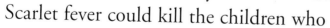

INFANT CLASSES

Morning lessons began at 9.45 and continued until midday, with a 15-minute play break at 10.45. Downstairs, in the infants' school, eight different classes were taught, each with about 60 to 70 children. They were taught to read and to count using wooden letters and numbers. They also sang the alphabet and chanted, 'One and one is two, one and two is three, one and three is four... ' Once they knew the alphabet, they learned to read simple textbooks.

▼ The infants drew, but they were not allowed to make up their own pictures. These infants are all copying a drawing from the board.

The youngest infants, the 'babies', were looked after by a 12-year-old girl monitor. Unlike the older children who had desks, they sat tightly packed on rising rows of benches, in a 'gallery'. This allowed the monitor to keep an eye on all of them. It also stopped the youngest children from falling off their seats and hurting themselves.

▼ This girl is learning to count. The wire circle she is holding has 18 beads – 6 colours arranged in groups of 3.

▲ A class of 'babies', or children under 5. The teacher has just asked them, 'Which is your right hand?' Can you spot the children who have fallen asleep?

In some infants' classrooms there was a cabinet of objects, which were brought out for 'object lessons'. An ordinary object, such as a lump of clay, a shoe or a glass, was handed to every child. The children then had to answer questions about it, such as 'What does it feel like?', 'What is it made of?' and 'What is it for?' This was the closest thing to science that many Victorian schoolchildren learnt.

MORNING LESSONS

Upstairs in the boys' school, morning lessons were under way. Each class had around 70 pupils. The big school rooms, shared by three classes, each held more than 200 boys. The only way that teachers could control such large numbers was to make sure that everyone did the same thing at the same time. The boys had to sit quietly at their desks until the teacher shouted an order, such as 'Take out slates!' or 'Open your books!' They were not allowed to speak unless spoken to. Boys who spoke in class or misbehaved were beaten with a cane.

◀ The boys of Standard Three, most of them aged 8 or 9, practise spelling on their slates. The assistant teacher reads out a passage from a book which the boys write down.

The same type of teaching was used in the girls' school. Victorian writers on education said that this strict method was especially good for poor children. It taught them 'cheerful obedience to duty', and so prepared them to work as servants, office clerks or factory workers.

Every now and then, a man turned up at the school gates dragging a miserable looking child. He was the attendance officer, nicknamed the 'kid catcher'. Every school board hired kid catchers to patrol the streets, rounding up children who played truant (stayed away from school).

◀ The attendance officer catches two boys who should be at school. These officers quickly learned the best places to track down children, such as Punch and Judy shows.

Boys and girls played truant for various reasons. Many were kept away from school by their parents, who wanted them to work or help around the house. In East London, children earned money making matchboxes. Their parents could be taken to court and fined for keeping children from school, but many could not do without the money earned by their children. In 1893, one mother explained, 'Of course we cheat the school board... It's hard on the little ones, but then their fingers is so quick.'

▼ A poor family making matchboxes in Bow, East London. Children were kept away from school to do a variety of jobs, including selling newspapers and shining shoes.

DINNER BREAK

At midday, the monitors rang hand-bells announcing the dinner break. The children of all three schools were ordered to stand at the sides of their desks. Then they were marched out of the building in single lines. For the next hour and a half, the children could play, watched over by a monitor or an assistant teacher with a whistle, who made sure that no fights broke out.

▼ Playtime in a London board school, around 1895. The children look very happy to be out of the classroom!

In the boys' playground, there were games of marbles, football, races with hoops, and chasing games, such as 'he'. Hoops were also popular in the girls' and infants' playground. The infants sat on the see-saw or played 'let's pretend' games, copying the behaviour of grown-ups.

Girls of seven and over played skipping and clapping games. There were dozens of different games. In 'Winding the Clock', for example, two girls spun the rope for a third, who had to turn in the air as she jumped, facing first one girl, then the other.

The board schools had no money for meals. Children were expected to bring bread and cheese with them, or go home for dinner. But the teachers soon noticed that many pupils had nothing to eat all day. To feed them, the schools turned to charity. Volunteers knocked on doors collecting money to buy food. Then they brought cooked meals to the school, serving them for a small sum. For a penny, you could have a plate of boiled meat and vegetables. If you couldn't afford a penny, you were given a free mug of soup. Often, this was just water in which some bones had been boiled, but it made a big difference to a hungry child.

▲ Volunteers serve a cheap meal of bread and soup to the poorest children.

◀ ▼ All sorts of games were played in the infants' playground. Can you identify any of these?

AFTERNOON LESSONS

Afternoon school began at 2 pm with another assembly and reading of the register. Then the children had two more hours of lessons. As in the morning, most of the lessons were in reading, writing and arithmetic. There were also a little geography and history. In the girls' school, there were sewing lessons, while the boys did drawings of simple objects, such as a bucket or a vase of flowers.

▼ The only physical exercise was called 'drill'. The children were made to jump, stretch and bend when the drill teacher shouted orders. They marched up and down the playground like soldiers. In fact, drill teachers were often retired army sergeants.

▼ In the 1880s, some school boards set up cookery centres. Here the girls could learn to make cheap but filling meals.

In Standard Four, the boys were taught a neat style of handwriting called 'copperplate'. They learned this by copying a sentence again and again. The sentence usually had a moral, such as 'Your aim in life should be a noble one'. Copperplate writing was needed for any office job. Although typewriters were beginning to be used, most letters and documents were still written by hand.

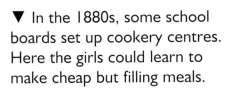

▼ In the 1890s, some board schools gave extra lessons on hygiene (health and cleanliness). These girls are being taught how to use a toothbrush. Tooth decay was very widespread, and almost everyone had to have rotten teeth pulled out.

INSPECTION DAY

There was one day every year which all the children and the teachers dreaded. This was the visit from the school inspector. He came to find out how well the school was doing its job. He checked through the registers to see how many children were coming to school. Then he tested all the pupils on their reading, writing and arithmetic.

These tests could be very difficult. Often, the inspectors read out passages for the children to write down which were full of unfamiliar words, and made little sense to them. For the children, passing meant moving up to a higher standard. Failure meant another year of the same lessons, and the shame of being in a class with younger children.

Teachers were under a lot of pressure to get good results from their pupils. The amount of money that the government paid each school depended partly on the inspection. If many children failed, the school's money was cut, and the teachers were paid lower wages.

◄ This 1886 cartoon shows children and teachers fleeing in terror when a frightening school inspector comes to visit their school.

THIS IS TO
CERTIFY THAT
E. Mansfield
attendances during
ending 28.4.1899
SNED R. H. Saunders
Printed in England

◄ The inspectors checked the number of times children were absent from school. Teachers tried to encourage children to come regularly by giving them attendance certificates, such as this one.

The inspector was also there to report on the staff. A bad report from the inspector could end a teacher's career. So the teachers were often just as scared of the inspectors as the children were.

In the days leading up to the inspection, the teachers tested the children again and again. When inspection day arrived, everyone was nervous. The children were confused by the change from the usual routine, and the teachers were worried that their pupils would do badly. Some schools taught the children a song to sing, to cheer them up and to impress the inspectors.

▲ The school inspectors question a child, while her teacher anxiously watches from the side.

THE END OF THE DAY

◀ When the monitor rang the bell to mark the end of lessons, the girls knelt at their desks and said a prayer together.

By 3.30 in the afternoon, the children were growing restless. They knew it was almost time to go home. They looked up at the clock on the wall every few minutes to see how much longer was left. At last, at 3.45, the monitors rang bells announcing the end of the school day.

When all the books and ink-wells were collected, prayers had to be said. In every room in the school, the children knelt at their desks, hands clasped, while their teacher said a short prayer. Then, at 4 pm, the teacher marched the children out by shouting orders. At the shout of 'One!', they all stood up. At 'Two!', they lifted one leg out of the desk. At 'Three!', the other leg followed. Then they had to march on the spot as the teacher chanted, 'Left, right, left, right.' A man called Joseph Ashby remembered what this felt like:

'It was agony – you were so longing to get outside. But if one boy pushed another you would have to go back and begin the rigmarole again.'

▼ After slipping their slates into the back of their desks, the girls were ordered to stand and march smartly out. They were free at last, until the next school day.

THE BOARD SCHOOLS

Do you think you would have liked going to a Victorian board school? Classes were very large, and many of them were taught by young monitors and pupil teachers. There was no attempt to make lessons interesting. Instead of letting children think for themselves, they were drilled to remember the answers to questions. But teachers and inspectors campaigned to change the schools. Classes became smaller and new ways of teaching were introduced. Eventually, they grew into our own primary schools. In fact, many Victorian board school buildings are still in use today.

PLACES TO VISIT

If you want to find out more about Victorian schools, why not visit one of these museums?

1 Angus Folk Museum, Glamis, Forfar, Tayside, DD8 1RT (tel. 0137 84288). A museum of nineteenth century life in Scotland, including education.

2 Industrial Museum, Eccleshill, Bradford, Yorkshire, BD2 3HP (tel. 01274 631756). Includes a display on education and a board school room.

3 North of England Open Air Museum, Beamish, County Durham, DH9 0RG (tel. 01207 231811). Visiting this museum, with its street of Victorian buildings, is like going back in time.

4 Ragged School Museum, Copperfield Road, London E3 4RR (tel. 0171 232 2941). Museum of life in the East End of London, including a schoolroom. Offers Victorian role-play lessons for groups of children.

5 St Johns House Museum, Warwick, Warwickshire, CV34 4NF (tel. 0926 412034). Museum of daily life in Warwickshire, including a Victorian schoolroom.

6 Ulster Folk and Transport Museum, Holywood, County Down, BT18 0EU (tel. 01232 428428). Reconstructed buildings, including a school, can be seen in this museum of daily life in Northern Ireland.

7 Weald and Downland Museum, Singleton, Sussex, PO18 0EU (tel. 01243 363348). Fascinating collection of historic buildings, including a small village school.

8 Welsh Folk Museum, St Fagans, Cardiff, CF5 6XB (tel. 01222 569441). Another collection of historic buildings, including a Victorian school.

INDEX

PICTURE ACKNOWLEDGEMENTS

ET Archive 10–11; Hulton Getty 18–19; Image Select 5, 13 top, 19 top, 20; Mansell Collection 12–13, 15, 16–17, 19 bottom; Mary Evans Picture Library 16 bottom; Robert Opie Collection 9, 21; Topham Picturepoint 8. The map on page 23 is by Peter Bull.